What Christians Should Know About...

Preparing for Christ's Return

Clive Corfield

Sovereign World

Scripture quotations are taken from
the HOLY BIBLE, NEW INTERNATIONAL VERSION.
© Copyright 1973, 1978, 1984 International Bible Society.
Published by Hodder & Stoughton.
Used by permission.

ISBN: 1 85240 266 0

SOVEREIGN WORLD LIMITED
P.O. Box 777, Tonbridge, Kent TN11 0ZS, England.

Typeset and printed in the UK by Sussex Litho Ltd, Chichester, West Sussex.

Acknowledgements

There are many to whom I am grateful for their help in writing this book. All those who form Sovereign Ministries who have patiently heard this message time and again and tirelessly travelled the length and breadth of this country as well as overseas, serving with me through the years. For your faithfulness, commitment, friendship and endurance I want to say thank you and to acknowledge that without you what has been accomplished would not have been. Your obvious devotion to Jesus shines through in all you do and in the way you do it. You know who you are, so be blessed. Even though we see together so much of God's manifest love and power, your greater reward is yet to come.

I would however like to specifically acknowledge Doreen Hodson for her text correction and typing. Alan Hodson for being such a good anchor man, and my wife Karen for her ability to juggle so many balls in the air (metaphorically speaking) and yet take time to turn my stammering gibberish into something reasonably coherent.

4

Contents

Introduction

As I look back over years of pastoral work and itinerant ministry, I have noticed how the Father at times puts a burning prophetic message in your heart which is carried wherever you go and shared at every given opportunity. It is both prophetic and relevant. 'Preparing for Christ's Return' is one such passionate message that burns within my own heart to share with those who will listen. We have held a series of one-day training seminars called 'Preparing the Bride' at St. Thomas' Church in Lancaster following this theme and now I feel it right to produce a booklet to make this teaching more widely available.

This message fits in very much with current themes of renewal and the anticipation of revival within our nation. There is so much talk about renewing love and intimacy with the Father and at the same time lives are being turned upside down as we are no longer able to continue in our old ways. There is a shaking, a renewing, and an emphasis focusing on the things of God's heart rather than on ourselves. It seems that out of the charismatic renewal there has evolved a very introverted and self-centred church and an abundance of teaching about God's healing and blessing. I believe the Lord is very much in this, but in addition He wants to bring a greater weight of maturity upon us and give us a clearer focus. We can then move on in our healing, taking our blessing into a place where we can achieve the objectives, purposes and plans of God and be captivated by the Father and what truly lies on His heart.

Just by way of information for those who have picked up this booklet and have no understanding of the names of the characters that I will be referring to:

The Lamb is the Lord Jesus Christ, also known as the bridegroom.
The Bride is the Church – those who know and love the Lord Jesus.

This booklet looks at an event about to take place, which is the return of Jesus Christ to this earth to take His bride unto Himself, and the process of the Holy Spirit's work in preparing the bride for that great event. I am not attempting to offer a theology on eschatology (the events of the end times), but I am hoping to stir the hearts of God's people to become aware of the enormous privilege of being alive today as we enter into times that previous generations have only dreamt of.

1

The Wedding of
the Lamb

Revelation 19 begins with a resounding chorus of the multitude of heaven shouting *'Hallelujah! Salvation and glory and power belong to our God'* and the host of heaven rejoicing over the destruction of the great prostitute, Babylon. We see significant personalities in heaven bowing down and worshipping God who is seated on the throne, a great multitude crying out *'Hallelujah! For our Lord God Almighty reigns.'* In verse 7 we read *'Let us rejoice and be glad and give Him glory! For the wedding of the Lamb has come and His bride has made herself ready. Fine linen, bright and clean, was given her to wear.* [Fine linen stands for the righteous acts of the saints] *Then the angel said to me "Write: 'Blessed are those who are invited to the wedding supper of the Lamb!'" And he added, "These are the true words of God."'*

We see three main things in this passage:

1. The wedding of the Lamb has come.

2. The Bride has made herself ready.

3. Blessed are those who are invited to the wedding.

Wherever I travel around the world there appears to be a heightened excitement and anticipation about the return of the Lord Jesus. This event, known as 'the parousia' which speaks of Christ's return, the literal presencing of Himself with us, is spoken of repeatedly throughout Scripture and is the great hope of the Church. Now, as never before, there seems to be a dawning of the reality of this event.

We may well fall out with each other, as theologians have done down through the centuries, about the sequence, timing, and detailed understanding of Jesus' return. One thing is sure though – Jesus *is* coming back again as a bridegroom for His bride and those who are in living relationship with Him through salvation are part of the bride.

2

The Three-stage Process
to Marriage

When Jesus walked this earth there were traditionally three stages to marriage. The first one was 'betrothal,' which was a legal agreement between the couple who were intending to marry. Even up to a generation ago when a man asked a young woman to marry him and she agreed, they became engaged or betrothed. This was a legally binding agreement, and if the man chose not to go through with the wedding it was possible for the girl to sue him for breach of contract. Therefore, we need to see marriage beginning at the time of betrothal as legal and binding. This gave security and assurance to the parties involved, sealing the relationship until the fulfillment of the forthcoming event – marriage.

The second stage was the coming of the bridegroom for his bride. We see this illustrated in Matthew 25 where Jesus tells the story of the parable of the virgins. In verse 6 we read *'At midnight the cry rang out: "Here's the bridegroom! Come out to meet him!"'* At this point the virgins, who were sleeping, woke up, trimmed their lamps and went out to meet the bridegroom and they formed the complete wedding party.

This led on to the third stage, which was the wedding feast – the actual joining of a husband and wife together and the accompanying celebration. The book of Revelation refers to this event taking place when the Church experiences the wedding supper of the Lamb.

> *'Then the angel said to me, "Write: 'Blessed are those who are invited to the wedding supper of the Lamb!'"'*
> (Revelation 19:9)

This three-stage process is also taking place in individual lives of believers. First of all there is a betrothal between Jesus and ourselves from the moment we are saved. When we give our lives to Him and submit to His Lordship, accept His forgiveness and cleansing through the power of the Cross, He enters into a legal contract with us. He says *'I will never leave you nor forsake you, I will be with you always, I will come again for you.'* We see this in John chapter 14. Jesus encourages us not to let our hearts be troubled but to trust in God and to trust in Him. When we are saved Jesus comes into our lives and we are sealed into Him. This relationship is legally binding, a covenant that is sealed with the blood of Jesus and the promise from Him that He will come for us.

The second stage of the process of marriage is the coming of the bridegroom for his bride. I believe this to be the return of the Lord Jesus from heaven to earth to take His bride, the Church, unto Himself.

The third stage is the completion of the marriage process. At the actual joining of the husband and wife, referred to as 'the wedding supper of the Lamb' there will be great celebration beyond our wildest dreams, a oneness with Him and with each other. We can only imagine what this wedding celebration will be like, but I know it will be far more glorious and wonderful than anything we have ever experienced here on earth.

What a privilege it is to be chosen to be part of the Bride of Christ. As a man, I find it quite difficult to see myself as a bride, especially the part about having to wear a white frilly dress and walking down the aisle! The whole concept of being a bride is difficult for men to grasp because of its feminine implication. However, if we can view it from the perspective that Jesus wants and loves us more than anything else in His creation and doesn't want to continue through eternity without us, that will give us some idea of the depth of His love, commitment and desire for us all.

When I first met Karen, my wife, it wasn't long into our acquaintance when I began to realise that I wanted to spend time in her company rather than in the company of others. As time progressed the desire in my heart for her far outweighed any practicality that may have been a hindrance or an obstacle. When

I had come to a point of not wanting to live without her I asked her to marry me, and to my delight she accepted. From that moment we were betrothed, planning and preparing for the wedding day itself. When we met at the church, we made our public vows before God and man and then entered into the celebration of the wedding reception. After that we went off to start our new life together as one. As the apostle Paul says in Ephesians 5, talking about marriage relationships, *'For this reason a man will leave his father and mother and be united with his wife, and the two will become one flesh. This is a profound mystery – but I am talking about Christ and the church.'* It seems that marriage on earth is a prophetic illustration of what is yet to take place with Christ and His Church. At this stage we are betrothed to Him and He promises to return for us and take us into the marriage supper of the Lamb, to become one and be complete with Him. For me and for many others, it is a great mystery that God would love me to the point of wanting to be in relationship with me. I would be grateful just to have eternal life and not be facing hell. It is incredible to me to think that we have been saved so that God might pour into us His love and blessing, as a loving bridegroom would want to love and cherish his new bride.

3

Preparation of
the Bride

'...For the wedding of the Lamb has come, and His bride has made herself ready' (Revelation 19:7)

I remember the day Karen and I married. I sat at the front of the church next to my brother, who was best man, waiting for my bride to arrive. The church was full of guests who had travelled the length and breadth of the country to be with us. Excitement filled the air as we awaited her arrival. It seemed like an eternity! Karen was only twenty minutes late but it seemed forever to me. Then suddenly the music struck up to announce her arrival, and we all stood and turned to greet her coming through the door of the church. I looked and saw a vision of beauty. Everything about her made my heart swell. Her dress was magnificent, her hair perfectly arranged and make-up expertly done, enhancing the natural beauty of her face. She was my bride and I so appreciated all the effort she had put into her preparation for this day.

Had Karen arrived wearing an old pair of Levi's, tatty trainers and with greens stuck between her teeth, I don't think I would have been quite so impressed, nor would I consider that the day meant anything of real importance to her at all. Praise God this was not the case!

As the time for the return of the Lord fast approaches there is a work that the Holy Spirit is doing in the bride to make her ready for her bridegroom.

Corporate Individuality

We have to view the Church, not only as a corporate body of

15

believers, but also as individual believers. The whole church is made up of individuals and therefore when the Bible speaks to us corporately it refers to us all individually as well. It is only when we as individuals start to change and become renewed that together we experience renewal. The tendency is for us to talk in corporate terms which often enables us to avoid personal responsibility, always waiting for 'them' and 'those people' to get their act together.

I believe there are three main ways in which the Holy Spirit is preparing the Church for the return of Jesus: the first is a call to holiness, the second is to live in wholeness, and the third is celebration, a prophetic foretaste of what is yet to come.

4

A Call to
Holiness

There have been many warnings of judgment on sin within the Church along with many promises of blessing and power. The following is a prophecy from a Pentecostal pastor, David Minor, written in 1987 that has been widely distributed throughout the Church. It is worth referring to it at this stage as I think it exemplifies the heart and intent of the Holy Spirit's work within the Church today:

'The Spirit of God would say to you that the wind of the Holy Spirit is blowing through the land. The Church, however, is incapable of fully recognising this wind. Just as your nation has given names to its hurricanes, so I have put my name on this wind. This wind shall be named 'Holiness unto the Lord'.

Because of a lack of understanding, some of my people will try to find shelter from the wind, but in so doing they shall miss my work. For this wind has been sent to blow through every church that names my name. It shall blow through every institution that has been raised in my name. In those institutions that have substituted their name for mine, they shall fall by the impact of my wind. Those institutions shall fall like a cardboard shack in a gale. Ministries that have not walked in uprightness before me shall be broken and fall. For this reason man will be tempted to brand this as a work of Satan, but do not be misled. This is my wind.

I cannot tolerate my Church in its present form, nor will I tolerate it. Ministries and organisations will shake and fall in the face of this wind and even though some will seek to hide from that wind, they shall not escape. It shall blow against your lives and all around you some will appear to be crumbling, and so they shall, but never forget this is my wind, says the Lord. With tornado force it will come and appear to leave devastation, but the Word of the Lord comes and says "Turn your face into the wind and let it blow." For only that which is not of me shall be devastated. You must see this as necessary.

Be not dismayed, for after this my wind shall blow again. Have you not read how my breath blew on the valley of dry bones? So it shall breathe on you. This wind will come in equal force as the first wind. This wind will also have a name. It shall be called 'The Kingdom of God.' It shall bring my power. The supernatural shall come in that wind. The world will laugh at you because of the devastation of the first wind. But they will laugh no more, for this wind will come with force and power that will produce the miraculous among my people and the fear of God shall fall on the nation.

My people will be willing in the day of my power, says the Lord. In my first wind that is upon you now I will blow out pride, lust, greed, competition and jealousy and you will feel devastated, but haven't you read 'Blessed are the poor in spirit for theirs is the kingdom of heaven'? So out of your poverty of spirit I will establish my kingdom.

Have you not read 'The kingdom of God is in the Holy Ghost'? So by my spirit my kingdom will be established and made manifest.

Know this also. There will be those who shall seek to hide from this present wind and they will try to flow with the second wind, but they will again be blown away by it. Only those who have turned their faces into the present wind shall be allowed to be propelled by the second wind.

You have longed for revival and a return to the miraculous and the supernatural. You and your generation shall see it, but it shall only come by my processes, says the Lord. The Church of this nation cannot contain my power in its present form. But as it turns to the wind of the Holiness of God, it shall be purged and changed to contain my glory.

This is judgment that has begun with the house of God, but it is not the end. When the second wind has come and brought in my harvest, then shall the end come.'

Hebrews 12 v 25-29 says, '*See to it that you do not refuse him who speaks. If they did not escape when they refused him who warned them on earth, how much less will we, if we turn away from him who warns us from heaven? At that time his voice shook the earth, but now he has promised "Once more I will shake not only the earth but also the heavens." The words "once more" indicate the removing of what can be shaken – that is, created things – so that what cannot be shaken may remain. Therefore, since we are receiving a kingdom that cannot be shaken, let us be thankful, and so worship God acceptably with reverence and awe, for our "God is a consuming fire."'*

We can see God is intent on bringing the Church into a place of true holiness, which is the very character of God. We have sung for a generation songs such as 'Refiner's Fire,' 'Search my heart Oh God,' 'I want to be like Jesus,' yet many of us have expected God to wave a magic wand over our heads and see holy stardust fall down to make us like Jesus. The reality is that the Holy Spirit will be a refining fire, He will be like wind blowing chaff away and He will test the true issues of the heart, because it is out of the heart that our motives, desires, behaviour and lifestyle emanate. He's calling the Church to repentance and exposing our true motives, our level of purity, integrity and general Christlikeness.

We are so often found to be wanting in these areas and yet God is offering a wonderful gift of repentance. Repentance always leads us to freedom, to wholeness and life, while self-justification will always lead us to death and bondage.

God is turning up the pressure in all of our lives and we are being shaken so that what does not reflect Christ and His kingdom will fall away and that which remains will be of value to Him. The sad reality is that many of us cling on to that which God has no real part in, and when His wind blows and shakes these things many will think it is the work of the devil and seek to preserve and protect that which God wants to destroy.

The wind of God not only shakes the things we build and create like structures, traditions, methods, and religious activities, but He will also shake our lives so that our true mettle can be revealed. God will do whatever it takes to get our attention on the issues that are important to Him, even if we think we have come to the end of our tether and are bewildered by our circumstances.

We may even try to rebuke the devil or blame others, when actually it is the hand of God bringing us to our knees in brokenness and true humility, so that the life of Christ might shine through us and not be filtered through our flesh.

Over the last decade we have seen the exposure of sin within international high profile Christian ministries. Men of God, who had enormous gifting, have been with prostitutes or involved in financial misdemeanours. Others continue in pride and arrogance, claiming that the end justifies the means as they control and dominate those under their leadership. The Lord is not so much interested in what He can do through us as what He can do *in* us. Gifting, no matter how great it is, is only an enabling by God to do things for the benefit of others and His glory. Let's face it, God spoke to one prophet through a donkey! He used the most reluctant of prophets, like Jonah, to achieve His own ends. There is very little that we have to glory in ourselves – He is after character, purity, holiness, true love and a motivation in our life and ministry inspired by the Holy Spirit. Our purpose must be to build the kingdom of God, not our own kingdom.

These are without doubt most challenging days. God is shaking, refining, blowing, causing the dross in our lives to come to the surface and be wiped off or blown away. This is what revival truly is – when God's people come in repentance, seeking God for who He is not for what they can gain from Him, but seeking His power and touch for a broken world so we may bring His healing to the nations.

2 Chronicles 7:14 illustrates this so well '...*If my people, who are called by My name, will humble themselves and pray and seek my face and turn from their wicked ways, then will I hear from heaven and will forgive their sin and will heal their land.*' The process for revival is quite simple: if God's people, who are called by His name, humble themselves, pray, seek the face of God, turn from **their** wicked ways (the emphasis is on **their** wicked ways) then God will hear from heaven, forgive **their** sins and begin to heal **their** land. The Church has a great responsibility to affect the spiritual climate of a nation. If we want to see God move in our nation, then we must first allow Him to move in our churches.

Unfortunately, there is so much ungodly control and quest for power that God is hardly allowed to be God within His Church. All too often man seeks to dictate to God what He and cannot do. As a result a battle is raging within the walls of churches throughout the land as to who is in control. It appears that God is demanding His church back from the control of man.

New Wine

The parable of wine and wineskins as told in Matthew 9:16-17 is so appropriate for us today. Without doubt the Father is pouring out the new wine of the Holy Spirit and is seeking new wineskins to contain what He is doing. The old skins have had their day. They were used to preserve the new wine of their time, but now the Holy Spirit is looking for hearts that are open to Him and willing to be flexible enough to work God's way today.

Jesus told us that we could not successfully sew a new patch onto an old piece of cloth because the stitching would tear. Likewise, the new wine can not be contained in old wineskins because both the old and the new will be ruined. Therefore true renewal is not a question of patching up the old or trying to bring the new into the old. Rather it is allowing the old to be renewed, to be restored and made new again.

God will not be mocked

God will not be mocked. He is beginning to expose the secret sins of our lives, showing the true motives of our hearts, calling the Church to holiness through repentance. There is no place to hide when the Holy Spirit begins to move. A farmer sifting his wheat needs a breeze to be blowing so that when he throws the whole grain into the air, the husk blows away leaving the kernel to fall to the ground. The husk is a hard protective shell around the kernel and I believe the kernel is what God wants to get to in our lives. The wind of the Holy Spirit is blowing away the hard husk of self-protection, self-righteousness, self-vindication, and self-justification. To be honest, most of us need this to be a sovereign work of God because we are often so deceived as to what is or isn't of God. We, like David in Psalm 51, must cry out *'Create in me a pure heart, O God'*, and it can only be a creative work of God to renew our hearts to be like His. We must therefore open ourselves up to the full strength of the wind of God blowing through our lives to cause the husks around us to be blown away. The pruned fruit of our lives will then fall into the hand of the Father so we can be available to fulfil His plans and purposes under His anointing according to His will and timing.

5

Healing

'The Spirit of the Sovereign Lord is on me, because the Lord has anointed me to preach good news to the poor. He has sent me to bind up the broken-hearted, to proclaim freedom for the captives and release from darkness for the prisoners, to proclaim the year of the Lord's favour and the day of vengeance of our God, to comfort all who mourn, and provide for those who grieve in Zion – to bestow on them a crown of beauty instead of ashes, the oil of gladness instead of mourning, and a garment of praise instead of a spirit of despair. They will be called oaks of righteousness, a planting of the Lord for the display of his splendour' (Isaiah 61 v 1-3)

As the earlier prophesy spoke of a first wind of the Holy Spirit called 'holiness' and a second wind called 'the kingdom of God,' I believe the refining work of the Holy Spirit will bring holiness to the Church. After that there will be an expression of the power of the kingdom of God as yet unknown in human history that will bring healing and wholeness. The passage above reflects the very heart and intent of God to bring abundant life to the earth, packed with miracles of healing and deliverance, confronting religiosity and bringing about true spiritual life.

Unfortunately, the reality is that we are often like the disciples who, although they had seen Jesus transfigured in glory on the mountain, still could not cast a demon out of a young boy due to their unbelief. The church, by and large, is impotent in the area of healing, deliverance and effective evangelism. I believe that following the refining wind of the Spirit there will come a move of God's power that to date we have been unable to handle due to our pride and self-centredness. It isn't until we love the broken and wounded in the same way that Jesus does, with the compassion of His heart, that we will begin to see the power of God moving.

We have to veer away from building our own ministry and move towards exercising the ministry of Jesus into the lives of others. We may have a comprehension of this, but God sees into our hearts. I believe there is a burning desire in the heart of the Father to touch the physically broken, damaged, wounded and the emotionally and mentally sick, with a power to heal and deliver that can only come from Him. This ministry is not an optional extra for the Church, but very much part of Her responsibility in bringing healing and full salvation to those within Her ranks.

It has been said that the Church is an army, a hospital and a family. I believe this is true, and each of us should find it a safe place to grow, learn and develop. We are called to be in an army that will touch the world for Jesus Christ and demonstrate the power of the kingdom of heaven. We are also called to be a hospital, though some like to live in hospital, constantly going from one sickness to another! Others only stay inside the family or army, serving or fighting, not realising that God has a greater purpose for them effected by the power of the cross.

I was speaking at a church on the south coast of England earlier this year and during the time of ministry a lady within the fellowship came forward to receive something from the Lord. As I was praying for her it became apparent that she could not hear, so I prayed that God would heal her ears in the name of Jesus. A couple of months after this event I received a letter from her saying she had been surprised I'd prayed for her hearing as she had never thought of asking God to heal her and thought it was something she just had to carry throughout her life. To her amazement, very early the following morning, the sound of the birds singing outside her bedroom window woke her up! God had gloriously and wonderfully healed her completely from her deafness.

Another lady I met a year or so ago had a background of witchcraft and had suffered severe mental and emotional damage. This dear lady had been receiving help from various people including a secular psychiatrist and Christian counsellors.

Although improvements had been made, she was still living in torment, fear and guilt. She had no real intimate relationship with God, although she knew He was her only hope. With the co-operation of the church, two of our team ministered to her, expelling the demonic and bringing healing to the damaged emotions, assuring her of forgiveness, acceptance, and building her up in the faith with the truth of God's Word. Within 36 hours this woman had been set free to such a measure that she could hardly contain her joy and liberty. As she began to tell others what God had done in her life, a broad smile on her face and a sparkle in her eyes demonstrated the power of God in setting captives free. It is the responsibility of the Church to bring healing to those who are saved, in every area of their being, and the Lord will work with those who are willing to work with Him in this regard.

6

Celebration

There has been a phenomenal outpouring of the Holy Spirit in recent years which has caused many people to be overcome with hysterical laughter, exhibit apparently drunken behaviour, light-heartedness, deep peace, assurance, security and a general blessing of the Father. To many folk this has been an offense and even thought by some to be demonic because it seemed inappropriate in a church setting. However, I believe it to be a prophetic foretaste of what is yet to come, an outpouring of the Father's blessing that is pointing us towards the return of Jesus to take His bride into the marriage supper of the Lamb. It will be the biggest party the world has ever seen and the greatest celebration of all time.

Even Jesus needed to keep His focus on the future in order to endure the sufferings of His day. Hebrews 12:2 tells us *'Let us fix our eyes on Jesus, the author and perfecter of our faith, who for the joy set before Him endured the cross, scorning its shame, and sat down at the right hand of the throne of God.'* How much more do we need a foretaste of the future to help us endure resistance to the gospel, persecution and evil, as well as the Refiner's fire. I think it's quite wonderful that the Holy Spirit should bring such a party to the Church. It's a little like Psalm 23 where David says *'He prepares a table before me in the presence of my enemies.'* If we are right in the midst of battle, facing our enemies, God prepares a banquet for us as a prophetic foretaste of what is yet to come. It will be the ultimate insult to the devil, an offense to the religious and an act of incredible faith when we can relax in the presence of the Father, trusting Him to be in control of His universe, whilst we soak in His love and grace. When we begin to rest in and enjoy the Father, the process of restoration and renewal of our lives is more effective, enabling us through the Holy Spirit to go back out into battle with our focus on the hope of the future, because we have had a prophetic foretaste of what is yet to come.

God is a Holy God and He is preparing His church to be holy for the return of the Lord Jesus. This is a prophetic foretaste of the holiness we shall know when we are one with Him. If healing and wholeness are part of our ministry, prophetically pointing towards complete wholeness in Christ, then, the Bible tells us, we will have incorruptible bodies that are like His and will be perfect as He is perfect.

There can also be a prophetic foretaste of celebration here on earth pointing towards what is yet to come, so we would do well to embrace what the Holy Spirit wants to do for us at any given time. If we are like the five *wise* virgins in the Matthew chapter 25 story referred to earlier, then we will have oil in our lamps burning brightly when the bridegroom comes to take us into the marriage supper of the Lamb.

7

Esther –
A Lesson in Preparation

The story of Esther was written around the fourth century before Christ, and is about God's providential care of His people. Although the name of God is not mentioned within the book, He is alluded to throughout it. Esther was a Jewish maiden who became Queen of Persia and was used to deliver her people from a massacre. The King of Persia, Xerxes, ruled over the known world at that time. His kingdom extended from India to Egypt and it was divided into 127 provinces. In the third year of his reign he gave a banquet for all his nobles, officials, military leaders and heads of the provinces. This was a grand affair and for 180 days he displayed the vast wealth of his kingdom.

After this was over a 7-day banquet began in the enclosed gardens of the King's palace. This banquet was open to all the people who lived in the citadel of Susa, from the least to the greatest. Decorations in the garden were quite elaborate, with hangings of white and blue linen fastened by cords of white and purple to silver rings on marble pillars. The couches on which they sat were of gold and silver. There was a mosaic pavement of marble, mother of pearl and other costly stones. The wine was served in golden goblets, each one being different from the next. There was an abundance of royal wine, in keeping with the King's liberality. He allowed each person to drink as much as he wanted and by and large it was a great time. Although Xerxes was not a worshipper of God, I feel that this is something of a picture of heaven with the great banquet celebrating the King, and with an extravagance of decoration, food and wine.

However, we read in the book of Esther that on the last day of the banquet the King invited his Queen, Vashti, to come and display her beauty to his guests. She refused to come in and instead held her own party. This obviously annoyed the King who sought advice from his counsellors. They said that they thought her behaviour might give wrong ideas to other women in the country and they too could start getting rebellious. The King's advisers therefore counselled him to be rid of Vashti and find another Queen, and Xerxes agreed. After some time the King's personal attendants proposed that a search be made for a beautiful young virgin for the King, and this is where Esther came into the story.

Esther, who had neither father nor mother, had been raised by her cousin, Mordecai, and they had been among the Jews taken into exile from Jerusalem to Babylon by King Nebuchadnezzar. Esther was very lovely in both form and features. Once the King's edict had been proclaimed, many girls were brought to the citadel of Suza and put under the care of Hegai, the master of the harem. Esther was one of these girls and because she pleased Hegai and won his favour, he rewarded her with beauty treatments, special food and assigned seven maids to her. We read that the King was very attracted to Esther and she won his favour and approval more than any other virgin, so he set his royal crown on her head and made her Queen instead of Vashti. The King then gave a great banquet for all his nobles and officials and proclaimed a holiday throughout the province, distributing gifts with royal liberality.

What can we learn from this story? First of all we learn that the King was extravagant, liberal, generous and wanted to share the riches of his kingdom with his subjects. Secondly, we see that although Queen Vashti was invited to join him in the celebrations to display her beauty to everyone gathered there, she refused and held her own party instead.

This reminds me of the story Jesus told in Luke 14:16 and Matthew 22:1-14 of the King who had prepared a wedding banquet for his son. He sent his servants to those who had already been invited to the banquet to tell them to come quickly as everything was now ready. Unfortunately those who had already been invited found other things to occupy their time. One said that he had just bought a field and must attend to it; another had bought five yoke of oxen and had to try them out; another had just got married and it appeared that his wife wouldn't let him come.

The servants returned to the King and informed him of their responses. The King ordered the servants to go out quickly into the streets and alleys of the town and bring in the poor, the crippled, the blind and the lame – all the people who thought they would never receive an invitation from a King. They were outcasts, the rejects of society, non-religious, unworthy, and yet the King preferred to have them rather than those who had been formally invited but rejected his invitation.

There was still room at the wedding feast, so the King then told his servants to go out into the roads and country lanes and compel people to come in so that his house might be full. The King was throwing a wide net and drawing in anyone who was willing to accept his free offer – after all, the hungry and the thirsty will always go where there is food and drink. The self-satisfied, preoccupied and self-sufficient prefer to carry on doing their own thing rather than enter into the will and desire of the King. So it was with Vashti, who preferred to hold her own party with her own friends doing her own thing, rather than responding in obedience to the King and entering into his celebration.

I am reminded too of Luke 15:11-31 when the prodigal son's brother refused to enter into his father's celebration for the younger son returning home. He was put-out and thought that the younger brother was unworthy, so refused to associate with him. In his own self-righteousness he remained outside the celebration refusing to share in his father's joy. We must note, however, both in Jesus' account of the King's banquet and the story of Vashti that the King rejected those who refused his invitation and instead searched for someone who would respond to him in the right way.

Responding to one another is essential for healthy relationships. It is only those who have an intimate relationship with a family or friend who get an invitation to a wedding and its subsequent celebration. We read in Revelation 19, *'Blessed are those who are invited to the wedding supper of the Lamb.'* This implies an existing intimacy and is a sign of friendship. We would only want those who are our friends and family to be at our wedding. It is often deemed an insult to refuse the honour and privilege of receiving such an invitation.

Returning to Esther's story, we notice that some rejected and some accepted the King's invitation to enter into his blessing and take part in his banquet. For those who accepted the invitation, like Esther, there was a period of preparation before presentation to the King. It took Esther twelve months of beauty therapy (six months of oil and myrrh and six months of perfumes and cosmetics)!

We know that oil is symbolic of the Holy Spirit. The oil speaks of the priestly anointing and of being soaked in the anointing power of the Holy Spirit. Myrrh has two symbolic implications: firstly, it was one of three ingredients used on the high priest's robes, mixed with aloes and cassia. This mixture was placed on the priest's garments and gave off a sweet fragrance. It was often possible to smell the priest coming before you could see him. Some have even noticed a beautiful fragrance when the anointed presence of the Lord Jesus comes into their midst. I believe it speaks of the priestly role of the Church as we stand between God and man and intercede for the world.

The second symbolic representation of myrrh is that of death. It was used in the preparation of bodies for burial. It speaks of death. It is true to say that we will never truly know resurrection life until there has been a death.

There is no other way into the abundant power of the Holy Spirit and knowing the effectual prayer of intercession until there has been a crucifixion of our flesh. 'Flesh' includes ambition, pride, ego and self-righteousness. John the Baptist declared that Christ must increase and that he must decrease. All too often people want power for their ministry and finance for their projects all in the name of Jesus. But is it for their own ambitious visions? We are forever seeking the hand of God and not His face. We rarely seek Him for who He is, rather than for what we can get out of Him.

God is putting to death works that only amount to wood, hay and stubble. He is putting to death works not born in the heart of God, but in the heart of proud and ambitious men and women using the name of God for their own ends. The Holy Spirit is working death in our flesh lives so that the life of the Spirit may have greater prominence. There is only one way to resurrection life and that is the way of the cross. Every other way is a deception!

After being soaked in oil and myrrh for six months, Esther undertook another six months of preparation treatment with perfumes and cosmetics. Now, my wife used to be a beauty therapist and over the years I have gained some insight into the use of cosmetics! What I have noticed is that they can enhance and highlight our good features to their best advantage, but can also camouflage blemishes that need to be hidden. To this end I can see the work of the Holy Spirit in our lives preparing us as the Bride of Christ, soaking us in His presence and drawing from us our true personalities in all their beauty and uniqueness. Those areas in our lives which are ugly due to sin, are covered with the blood of Jesus, bringing cleansing and healing to the our damage with His grace and mercy. Instead of exaggerating these damaged areas, they are camouflaged until the recovery process has been completed and they can be included in the whole picture. Then the 'cosmetics' of God can highlight our healed and whole personality to its full potential, thus glorifying God and displaying His work of grace and love.

We note too that Esther was given special favour and won the approval of those attending her before she was presented to the King. This speaks of God's grace, generosity, and the richness and abundance of His favour towards us if we are willing to receive the ministry of God's love into our lives – allowing Him to beautify us before we are presented to the King.

I believe we are entering into a time of the fulfilment of Isaiah 61:2, which says this is '...*the year of the Lord's favour*' – a time when we can experience God's blessing instead of labouring under the curse of death which religion often brings. It is now time to move into the blessing of God and allow Him to minister His love and healing into our lives through intimacy. Like Esther we too feel we are orphans, abandoned and rejected. Now the Father calls us into His palace right up to His banqueting table, where we may know we are loved and accepted as we are, not as we ought to be.

This whole process of being refined and knowing more of His abiding presence, which at times is like being soaked with His oil and myrrh and at other times like being worked on with perfumes and cosmetics, is all part of the preparation of the bride. This procedure causes the features of our personality to be impregnated with Him so that His glory is manifest in our lives.

8

First Love

Part of the process of God preparing the bride is to bring us into a new level of intimacy and relationship with the Lord Jesus. During this time of betrothal we can discover more about Him, His ways, plans and purposes, so that we too can share in His heart's desires as we grow closer to Him and become more like Him.

Jesus often made startling statements that at times brought offence to the hearers, but His words were always meant to challenge, to provoke thought and to bring change within the lives of those who were listening. One such occasion is found in Matthew 18 when the disciples had come to Jesus asking who was to be the greatest in heaven. Jesus' response was to take a little child and have him stand among them, then say *'I tell you the truth, unless you change and become like little children, you will never enter the kingdom of heaven. Therefore, whoever humbles himself like this child is the greatest in the kingdom of heaven.'* Three words come out of this passage like a light in the darkness: *change ... humble... child.*

First of all we have to look at this word 'change' which means to repent. It is like going along one path, changing your mind and going back along the way you came. Jesus offers this challenge to all of us, where there is a need for us to change, to repent. The second word to consider is 'humble.' We read in James 4:6 (who quotes from Proverbs 3:34) *'God opposes the proud but gives grace to the humble.'* This means that God is diametrically opposed to those who have a proud heart, no matter how right they are, how correct their theology, doctrine, practice or tradition. However, He gives grace to the humble, even though they may have imperfect theology, deficient practice and no tradition. This is a tremendous challenge to many of us because we have been so proud of our correctness, our accomplishments, our systems and visions. We may find that God has set His face directly to oppose us because of the issues of our hearts, while often the inefficient or uneducated can be experiencing the grace and favour of God because of the condition of their humble hearts.

The third word that shines out of this passage, is 'child.' We are told to humble ourselves like a child and it seems our measure of childlikeness is linked to our stature in the kingdom of heaven. There is an initial contradiction here though. God calls us to maturity and yet calls us to be childlike. He calls us to grow up and yet to be like a child. Well, it may be that God is not advocating childishness in the sense of immaturity, which is unfortunately predominant in certain sections of the church, but rather *childlikeness*. A healthy child in a secure environment will be very trusting, will depend upon his or her parents, and be vulnerable, playful, innocent, teachable, meek, spontaneous, impulsive and aware of what is happening around them. Maybe we have lost these childlike qualities in our walk with the Lord and have become self-dependent, self-protective, mistrusting, unteachable, proud and have perhaps forgotten how to play and enjoy our Christian life. We may have lost spontaneity and impulsive responses to the things of the Spirit of God and become grown-up, controlling adults who think they know best.

The challenge Jesus brings is that unless we *change* and become like *children again* through the process of *humility* we will never enter the things of the kingdom of heaven.

Jesus was once challenged by the religious people of His day who asked what was the greatest of all the commandments. He responded by quoting Deuteronomy 6:5 *'Love the Lord your God with all your heart and with all your soul and with all your strength." This is the first and greatest commandment. And the second is like it: "Love your neighbour as yourself." All the law and the Prophets hang on these two commandments.'* In other words by loving God and experiencing His love for us and loving our neighbour as we love ourselves we are fulfilling the law of God. It is as simple as that. Everything in the Christian faith hangs on this command, yet we have complicated our Christian lives and allowed other issues and circumstances to cloud our vision of Jesus. This then causes us to veer away from His primary objectives for our lives. In a sense we have gone off at a tangent away from loving God and loving each other.

In Revelation chapter 2 we see a letter which Jesus wrote to the Ephesian church. Now it has to be said that this church at Ephesus was a solid church. Our Lord commends them for their perseverance, for enduring hardships, their hard work, the fact that they didn't tolerate wickedness, and that they tested false apostles. In verse 4, however, we read *'Yet I hold this against you: you have forsaken your first love',* or as the New Living Translation puts it, *'You don't love me or others as you did at first.'* Jesus goes on to challenge them to remember the height from which they had fallen, to repent (change), and do the things they did at first (childlikeness). The solemn warning continues, saying that if they do not repent and do what they did at first, then He would come and remove their 'lampstand from its place.' The word of God is true and we are warned that God resists the proud but gives grace to the humble.

As in the Ephesian church, it may be that we too have lost that first love. We have been preoccupied with preserving truth, enduring hardships, resisting wickedness, working hard, and testing that which appears to be false within the Church. But our time may have become so absorbed by the devil and warfare that we have been chasing our tails and forsaken the most important commandment of all, to love God and allow Him to love us. Instead of us pulsating with the love and vibrancy of the Holy Spirit, many of us have become bankrupt on the inside, trying to perform to gain God's approval and the approval of others.

There is a desperate need for us to know the love of God in Christ Jesus again, to melt away the ice and hardness that has gripped our hearts and hinders us from hearing the things of the Spirit. Jesus challenges us to remember where we have come from and repent again, humbling ourselves and becoming childlike again – spontaneous, impulsive, meek, teachable, playful, vulnerable, dependent upon Him. If we fall in love with Jesus again He will reveal His love for us, but if we do not, the lampstand (the presence of God) that is ours will be removed from its place.

There is strong biblical basis for acknowledging that God will remove His abiding presence if we turn away from Him and fail to follow His ways. Not least of all the tragic story of when Israel lost the Ark of the Covenant to the Philistines during the days of Eli the priest (1 Samuel chapter 4). Eli had failed to discipline his sons for their contemptable behaviour and therefore God allowed the Ark to be captured. The Ark represented the abiding presence of God in the midst of them. Not only was the Ark taken into enemy hands which in itself brought shame and disgrace, but the Philistines also inflicted an enormous defeat upon the Israelites. More than 30,000 soldiers died and the remaining men fled to their own tents. In the process Eli's two sons were killed. When Eli heard of this he was so shocked at the news that he fell backwards off his chair, broke his neck and died. His daughter-in-law was pregnant. When she heard that her husband and father in law were dead and that the Ark had been captured she went into labour. Although she gave birth to a son she was overcome by her labour pains and died. Before she died she named the boy Ichabod (meaning 'no glory'), saying, 'The glory of the Lord has departed from Israel.'

As the presence of the Lord departs, so His protective, providing blessings go with Him, leaving only curse and consequence to contend with. Just as Vashti was rejected and those who had been invited to the King's Banquet were also rejected, so too its possible that we can be rejected because we lose our first love. Jesus said that unless we repent He will come and take our lampstand from its place. Revelation 2:7 says, *'He who has an ear, let him hear what the Spirit says to the churches.'*

Love is a priority for God – to love us and have us loving Him is what He desires more than anything else. Very often we hold God at a distance by acknowledging His majesty, greatness and might, yet when Jesus came to earth He was known as **Emmanuel** (meaning 'God with us') which shows His desire to be intimate, accessible, and someone with whom we can have a relationship. We know too that Jesus tended to work **with** God rather than **for** God. We see in John 5:19 that Jesus only did what He saw the

Father doing. In John 12:49 we read that Jesus only said what He heard the Father saying.

At all times it appears that Jesus operated from a position of rest. Psalm 46:10 says *'Be still and know that I am God.'* It is so hard for us in our modern world of activity and pressure just to be still and know Him and know about Him. To know Him in intimacy and give time to renew that relationship. Ephesians 3:17-21 tells us that we are rooted and established in love. *God is love.* We have a theology of it, but very often we have little experience of it. Christ, the Bridegroom, is coming for the Church, His bride. This is romance of the highest order. However, many in the church find it so difficult to love either the unsaved or the unlovely, because they cannot love or accept themselves – often because they in turn have not yet been loved.

'We love because He first loved us' (1 John 4:19) and we desperately need this revelation of His love so that we might be healed in our hearts, receive His acceptance and learn to accept ourselves. We can then in turn begin to love and accept others. So much ministry and activity within the Church is motivated by guilt and pressure rather than a motivation of the Father's love operating in and through us. It is time to change!

The Christian life is one of *relationship* – the bride with her bridegroom – this is an issue of the heart. Matthew 15:8-9 declares, *'These people honour me with their lips, but their hearts are far from me. They worship me in vain; their teachings are but rules taught by men.'* Our churches are full of people who honour God with their lips, with their time, with their work, with their effort, *but their hearts are far from Him*. They worship God's word rather than coming to Him so they might have life. Many of us have forsaken intimacy with Jesus because we have dogmatically followed teachings that are nothing more than rules taught by men. If that is the case then there will be no love, no intimacy, no relationship with the Saviour Himself.

Jesus said, *'You diligently study the Scriptures because you think that by them you possess eternal life. These are the Scriptures that testify about me, yet you refuse to come to me to have life'* (John 5:39). Many of us have forsaken intimacy with the person Jesus and tended to worship our doctrine. Instead of loving God we have loved the Bible and treated the Scriptures in an idolatrous way, elevating them above a relationship with Jesus and suffering the inevitable consequences of such idolatry. The Bible is a revelation and a signpost to the person Jesus, it is our relationship with Him that is paramount.

The Bible enables us to know Him and understand His ways. It is not God itself, although it is revered as such in some circles.

We have replaced parts of the Godhead with things that are valuable to us but are not God themselves. They are often things that have become idolatrous in our lives. We are called to worship God the Father, Son and Holy Spirit. However, we may worship God the Father, Son and God our doctrine, or God the Father, Son and God our tradition. Even our ministry, denomination, gifts and calling can replace the very intimacy with the Father for which we were created and redeemed to enjoy and participate in. They can become the very driving force of our lives and the object of our passion. The Holy Spirit is calling us back to intimacy with Jesus.

There is a passage of scripture that highlights the condition of much of the Church today. It is found in Song of Solomon chapter 5 and tells of a bride who is awakened by her lover, her bridegroom, knocking on the door. He says to her *'Open to me, my sister, my darling, my dove, my flawless one. My head is drenched with dew, my hair with the dampness of the night. I have taken off my robe – must I put it on again? I have washed my feet – must I soil them again?'*

It appears that the bride doesn't open the door but remains in what I might suggest as a self-satisfied state imagining what it would be like for the bridegroom to come in and love her. She doesn't respond, so he knocks again and this time thrusts his hand through the latticework in an attempt to operate the lock from the inside. She tells of how her heart began to pound for him and her hands dripped with myrrh (remember Esther). When she eventually went to open the door the lover had gone because she was too slow to respond to him. Her heart sank at his departure and she ran out looking for him but could not find him. It was late and the watchman who saw her mistook her for a woman of the night by reason of the way she was dressed and abused her.

What a tragic story! The bride was longing for her husband and the husband was longing for his bride but she would not respond to him by opening the door. No matter what his desire for her was and what attempts he made to get in, only she had the right to open the door and let him in. Instead of just imagining what it would be like she could have known him and experienced his love, but instead she ended up being damaged and abused by those who misunderstood her.

In a similar way Jesus speaks very clearly to us in Revelation 3:20, a text often used in evangelism that was never written to the unsaved, but rather to the church in Laodicea, God's own people. This church was described as neither hot nor cold, who thought they were rich but were spiritually barren. They had accumulated material assets but were spiritually bankrupt, naked, blind, deaf and couldn't see or hear what God was seeking to communicate. They were neither one thing nor the other, just nominal, and gave allegiance to God with their lips but their hearts were far from Him. God in His love and mercy therefore cries out to them, *'Here I am! I stand at the door and knock. If anyone hears my voice and opens the door, I will come in and eat with him and he with me.'* Just like the bride in the Song of Solomon the operation of the door of our hearts can only be done from the inside. Jesus is knocking on the door of our hearts, saying 'Here I am, will you let me in?' Church, if we don't let Jesus into our hearts and allow Him rule and reign there, we might be rejected because we have lost our first love. We have to let Him be God over our lives, giving Him permission to flood us with His love, grace and mercy, to radically change us and ruin us for anything other than Himself. If we make Him remain outside, He may well remove His presence.

The call of God to this generation is therefore to renew that first love of Him, repent of our ungodly control and allow Him, the King of Glory, to come in to love us, heal us, renew us, restore us, and fill us with the power which comes from His spirit alone. We will then be in a position to offer to the world what we ourselves have received, but until we have received it ourselves we will have very little to give to others.

Conclusion

Jesus is coming again and the Father has released the Holy Spirit to prepare the bride – *us* – for the return of His son Jesus. He is purging, cleansing and calling us to holiness while healing us on the inside and in our physical bodies. He is giving us a foretaste of the celebration of heaven here on earth and is inviting us all to join in the party. He desires to soak us in His love and anointing so that we can have our first love renewed. Instead of trying to gain His approval and acceptance, we can, from a position of security and assurance, serve Him to fulfill His plans and purposes. Are you willing to change, humble yourself and become childlike in your responses to God, so that He might prepare you to meet with Him?

1 Thessalonians 4:13-18 says *'Brothers, we do not want you to be ignorant about those who fall asleep, or to grieve like the rest of men, who have no hope.' We believe that Jesus died and rose again and so we believe that God will bring with Jesus those who have fallen asleep in Him. According to the Lord's own Word, we who are still alive and are left till the coming of the Lord, will certainly not precede those who have fallen asleep. 'For the Lord Himself will come down from heaven with a loud command, with the voice of the archangel and with the trumpet call of God, and the dead in Christ will rise first. After that, we who are still alive and are left will be caught up together with them in the clouds to meet the Lord in the air. And so we will be with the Lord forever. Therefore encourage each other with these words.'*

'He who testifies to these things says "Yes, I am coming soon." Amen. Come, Lord Jesus'   (Revelation 22:20)

You may contact the author by writing to:

Sovereign Ministries
P.O. Box 112
Lancaster
LA1 5GG
England

Tel/Fax: (0)1524 382141
Email: sovmin@aol.com

❖   ❖   ❖   ❖

If you have enjoyed this book and would like to help us to send a copy of it and many other titles to needy pastors in the **Third World**, please write for further information or send your gift to:

Sovereign World Trust, P.O. Box 777, Tonbridge, Kent TN11 0ZS, United Kingdom

or to the **'Sovereign World'** distributor in your country.

Other titles available in the 'What Christians Should Know About....' series:

Depression Anxiety, Mood Swings
and Hyperactivity
By Dr. Grant Mullen

The Endtime Harvest
By David Shibley

Escaping From Debt
By Keith Tondeur

Generational Sin
By Pennant Jones

The Glory of God
By Ed Roebert

How to Pray Effectively for Your
Lost Loved Ones
By David Alsobrook

The Importance of Forgiveness
By John Arnott

A Personal Relationship with God
By Peter Nodding

Preparing for Christ's Return
By Clive Corfield

Reconciliation
By John Dawson

Sickness and Healing
By Ed Harding

Their Value to God
By Steve and Chris Hepden

Power Filled Worship
By Russ Hughes